The Family Kitchen
SMALL BITES

Contents

hinkler

Published by Hinkler Books Pty Ltd
45–55 Fairchild Street
Heatherton Victoria 3202 Australia
www.hinkler.com.au

Text and images © Anthony Carroll 2010
Design and layout © Hinkler Books Pty Ltd 2013
Page layout: Dynamo Limited
Prepress: Splitting Image

ISBN: 978 1 7430 8336 9

Printed and bound in China

Introduction

Finger foods and small bites are perfect for parties. Whether slurped off a shell or spoon, dipped and then crunched, or snacked upon in one hand with a glass of wine in the other, there seems to be no end to the ways we can enjoy these delectable tidbits. Plus, the preparation is mostly done in advance, so there is little to clean up afterwards.

Next time you entertain, ditch the uninspired chips and nuts. Instead, impress your friends with some smart canapés that will keep the wolf from the door during pre-dinner drinks. Finger foods can serve as an appetiser before a traditional seated main meal, or become the meal itself. Be inventive and host a cocktail-style dinner party, with a tasting menu of bite-sized morsels. Start with a dip and end with a miniature dessert or two – and with the help of this book, there are endless possibilities in between.

Asian cuisines come into their own with the cooking of small bites. Choose from Teriyaki, Chilli and Ginger Oysters, Crab Rice Paper Rolls, Duck Pancakes, Chicken Yakitori, Mini Beef Satays, Honey Glazed Spare Ribs or Japanese Pork Gyozas. Why not throw an oriental-themed party and serve a selection of these tasty treats?

Don't forget that a few finger foods can also become a delicious low-fuss meal for a quiet night with friends in front of the TV. Some of these recipes only take minutes to put together and don't require any cooking, so there's no reason why they shouldn't become a regular part of your culinary repertoire.

Pâtés, Dips and Spreads

It's surprisingly easy to make classic dips and spreads like Tapenade, Guacamole and Chicken Liver Pâté. You'll find fresh ideas here, too, such as Beetroot Tzatziki and the nachos-inspired Mexican Layered Dip.

Chicken Liver Pâté

Serves 4 · Preparation and cooking 20 minutes

125g (4½oz) butter

1 onion, finely chopped

1 clove garlic, finely chopped

1 rasher bacon, finely chopped

250g (9oz) chicken livers, cleaned

½ teaspoon fresh thyme, chopped

salt and freshly ground black pepper

1 tablespoon brandy

¼ cup cream

1 packet water biscuits (crackers) or mini toasts

1 Melt butter in a frying pan (skillet), add the onion, garlic and bacon and cook until tender. Add chicken livers, thyme, salt and pepper. Cook a further 5 minutes.

2 Allow to cool slightly then place in a food processor and process until smooth. Add brandy and cream and process until well combined.

3 Place into a serving bowl and surround with water biscuits (crackers) or mini toasts.

Fish Pâté

Serves 6 · Preparation and cooking 20 minutes + several hours chilling

500g (1 lb) fish fillets, skinned

1 spring (green) onion, finely chopped

2 strips lemon peel, finely chopped

125ml (4¼fl oz) dry white wine

1 chicken stock (bouillon) cube

60g (2oz) butter

salt and cayenne pepper

85ml (2¾fl oz) cream

2 teaspoons lemon juice

1 packet crispbread or toasted bread

1 Place fish fillets, onion, lemon peel, wine and stock (bouillon) cube into a frying pan (skillet). Simmer gently for 5 minutes or until fish is just tender. Drain fish fillets, reserving liquid. Remove and discard any bones from fillets.

2 In a food processor, place boned fish, reserved liquid, butter, salt, cayenne pepper, cream and lemon juice and purée until smooth.

3 Spoon into a serving bowl or individual moulds. Refrigerate for several hours. Serve with crispbreads or toasted bread.

Mexican Layered Dip

Serves 12 · Preparation and cooking 1 hour + 1 hour chilling

500g (1lb) can refried beans

225g (8oz) beef mince (ground beef)

225g (8oz) spicy pork sausage

1 medium onion, chopped

½ teaspoon salt

½ teaspoon chilli powder

½ teaspoon ground cumin

100g (3½oz) green chillies, drained

125g (4½oz) cheddar (American) cheese, grated

1 cup medium or hot taco sauce

185ml (6¼fl oz) sour cream

spring (green) onions, chopped, for garnish

125g (4½oz) pitted black (ripe) olives, sliced

125g (4½oz) stuffed green olives, sliced

2 packets crackers

1 Put the beans in the bottom of a casserole dish at least 23cm (9in) in diameter.

2 Brown the beef, sausage and onion in a frying pan (skillet), season with salt, chilli powder and cumin. Drain, and distribute evenly over the beans. Cool slightly. Chop the green chillies, reserving a few pieces for garnish, and place the balance over the meat.

3 Spread the grated cheese over the dish. Top with taco sauce. Refrigerate at least 1 hour to let the flavours blend.

4 At serving time, preheat the oven to 200ºC (180ºC fan, 400ºF, gas 6) and bake the dip for 30–35 minutes. Top with spoonfuls of sour cream, garnish with spring (green) onions and olives and serve with a selection of crackers.

Guacamole

Serves 4–6 · Preparation 10 minutes

3 ripe avocados

juice of ¼ lemon

1 small onion, finely chopped

1–2 fresh chillies, finely chopped

2 garlic cloves, crushed

100ml (3½fl oz) crème fraîche

salt and freshly ground black pepper

1   Use a fork to blend the avocado flesh with the lemon, onion, chilli, garlic and crème fraîche. Season with salt and pepper and pour into bowls.

Horseradish Dip

Serves 4–6 · Preparation 10 minutes

250g (8oz) fresh curd cheese

3 tablespoons horseradish, grated fresh or bottled

horseradish sauce

50g (1½oz) chives, finely chopped

¼ teaspoon herb salt

1   Mix all ingredients thoroughly and pour into a bowl.

Tapenade

Serves 6–8 · Preparation and cooking 35 minutes + 2 days chilling

300g (10½oz) black (ripe) olives

100g (3½oz) anchovies

200g (7oz) capers

1 clove garlic, crushed

100–200ml (3½–7fl oz) olive oil

1 teaspoon French mustard

lemon juice

fresh basil, finely chopped

freshly ground black pepper

Toast

thinly sliced day-old bread

1 clove garlic

olive oil

1 Drain olives and remove pips. Drain anchovies. Place the olives, anchovies, capers and garlic in a blender. While the blender is running, add drops of olive oil and continue until the mix is smooth. Season with mustard, lemon, basil and black pepper.

2 Keep refrigerated in a glass jar and let it mature for a couple of days.

3 Preheat the oven to 190ºC (170ºC fan, 375ºF, gas 5). Gently rub the slices of bread with a cut clove of garlic and brush with olive oil. Bake for about 10–15 minutes, turning halfway through the cooking time, until the bread is golden brown.

4 Spread a spoonful of the mix onto each slice of toast and serve.

Beetroot Tzatziki

Serves 4–6 · Preparation 10 minutess

200ml (7fl oz) plain yoghurt

4–5 small pickled beetroot, grated

150g (5oz) fetta cheese, mashed

1 onion, finely chopped

1 teaspoon salt

¼ teaspoon freshly ground black pepper

1 Mix all ingredients thoroughly and pour into a bowl.

Sweet-chilli Dip

Serves 4–6 · Preparation 10 minutes

200ml (7fl oz) plain yoghurt

100ml (3½fl oz) sweet-chilli sauce

1 garlic clove, crushed or finely chopped

¼ bunch parsley, chopped

1 Mix all ingredients thoroughly and pour into a bowl.

Ham Hock Spread

Serves 4 · Preparation 10 minutes

1 cup smoked ham hock (flesh only), finely shredded

2 teaspoons horseradish, freshly grated, or bottled horseradish sauce

½ cup cream cheese

2 tablespoons crème fraîche

chopped chives

salt and freshly ground black pepper

1 Bind meat together with the horseradish, cheese and crème fraîche. Add chopped chives and season with salt and pepper.

2 Serve with crackers or chunky slices of bread and garnish with flat-leaf parsley, chopped chives or fresh dill (dill weed).

Salmon Spread

Serves 4 · Preparation 10 minutes

Salmon sauce

3 tablespoons sweet mustard

1 tablespoon French mustard

1 egg yolk

2 tablespoons white (granulated) sugar

2 tablespoons white wine vinegar

200ml (6¾fl oz) olive oil

Salmon spread

5 slices smoked salmon

2–3 tablespoons salmon sauce

1 tablespoon dill (dill weed), freshly chopped

freshly ground black pepper

1 To make the sauce, mix all the sauce ingredients thoroughly.

2 Cut the salmon into thin shreds and bind it with the sauce. Season with dill (dill weed), freshly ground pepper. Serve with crackers or chunky slices of bread and garnish with flat-leaf parsley, chopped chives or fresh dill.

Ginger Crab Spread

Serves 20 · Preparation 6 minutes

170g (6oz) can crabmeat

1 tablespoon crushed ginger (gingerroot)

⅓ cup mayonnaise

salt and freshly ground black pepper

1 packet of crispbread

10 pickled cucumbers (gherkins), halved lengthways

parsley to garnish

1 Place crabmeat, ginger (gingerroot), mayonnaise and salt and pepper in a food processor and process into smooth paste.

2 Spread a layer of the paste on the crispbreads and place a half of pickled cucumber (gherkin) on top of each. Garnish with a sprig of parsley and serve on a platter.

Vegetarian

Take a tour around Europe with Spinach and Fetta Filo Pastry Parcels from Greece, Mozzarella and Tomato Skewers with Basil Oil — a twist on the classic Italian salad, and a French favourite, Cheese-filled Petits-choux.

Cheese-filled Petits-choux

Makes 20–25 · Preparation and cooking 35 minutes

Choux pastry

1 cup water

4 tablespoons butter

1 cup plain (all-purpose) flour

3 eggs, beaten

Filling

250g (8oz) fresh curd cheese

¼ bunch chives, chopped

¼ bunch parsley, leaves picked and chopped

1 clove garlic, crushed

2–3 tablespoons crème fraîche

salt and freshly ground black pepper

parsley leaves to garnish

1 Preheat oven to 200ºC (180ºC fan, 400ºF, gas 6).

2 Place water and butter in a saucepan and cook over gentle heat until butter has melted and water boils. Remove from heat, add the sifted flour and stir vigorously.

3 Return to heat and stir continuously until mixture forms a ball around the spoon. Cool. Gradually beat in the eggs, beating well between each addition.

4 Place teaspoons of mixture onto greased baking trays (sheets) and sprinkle trays with cold water. Bake at 200ºC (180ºC fan, 400ºF, gas 6) for 10 minutes, reduce heat to 180ºC (160ºC fan, 350ºF, gas 4) and continue to cook for a further 30 minutes or until puffs are golden and feel light in the hand. Pierce puffs to allow steam to escape. Allow to cool.

5 Mix cheese, herbs, garlic and crème fraîche until smooth and creamy. Add salt and pepper to taste.

6 Fill the petits-choux and garnish with the parsley leaves.

Cherry Tomatoes with Artichoke Filling

Makes about 60 · Preparation and cooking 20 minutes

3–4 punnets cherry tomatoes

Artichoke filling

400g (14oz) artichoke hearts

125g (4½oz) parmesan cheese, grated

250ml (8½fl oz) mayonnaise

¼ cup fresh parsley, chopped

1 Cut a slice off the bottom of each washed tomato. Carefully remove the seeds and allow the tomato to drain upside down on paper towels.

2 Drain the artichoke hearts. In a blender or food processor chop them finely. Add the cheese and mayonnaise to the artichokes and blend well.

3 Fill each tomato using either a an icing (pastry) bag fitted with a large tip or a very small spoon. Cover the tomatoes and refrigerate. At serving time the tomatoes may be served at room temperature, or heated for 5 minutes in a 90ºC (80ºC fan, 195ºF, gas ¼) preheated oven. Garnish with a sprinkle of chopped parsley.

Cheese and Olive Muffins

Makes 15–20 · Preparation and cooking 40 minutes

300g (10½oz) plain (all-purpose) flour

½ teaspoons baking powder

¼ teaspoon salt

¼ teaspoon garlic pepper

100g (3½oz) parmesan cheese, grated

100g (3½oz) mixed olives, pitted and halved

2 eggs

2 tablespoons oil

⅓ cup natural yoghurt

fresh herbs for garnish

1 Preheat oven to 220ºC (200ºC fan, 430ºF, gas 7). Mix flour, baking powder, salt, grated cheese and olives in a bowl. Make certain the olives are coated in flour. Whip together eggs, oil and yoghurt. Stir into the flour mix. Stir thoroughly and distribute the mix in dollops into the patty cases using a small spoon.

2 Bake in the lower part of the oven for approximately 10–15 minutes. Serve with a dip or good quality butter.

Mozzarella and Tomato Skewers with Basil Oil

Makes approximately 20 · Preparation 10 minutes

1 small bunch of fresh basil

100ml (3½fl oz) olive oil

salt and freshly ground black pepper

20 cherry tomatoes, halved

20 mozzarella balls (bocconcini)

1   Run the basil in the blender together with the olive oil and season with salt and pepper.

2   Thread the tomatoes and mozzarella balls (bocconcini) on toothpicks, add a few drops of the sauce and serve on a plate.

Small Crostini with Tomato, Basil and Avocado

Makes about 15–20 · Preparation and cooking 20 minutes

6 firm tomatoes

1 bunch fresh basil, finely chopped

1 garlic clove, finely chopped

olive oil

a few drops white wine vinegar

salt and freshly ground black pepper

1 avocado

1 small baguette

25g (1oz) butter

extra garlic clove

1 Cut the tomatoes into wedges and remove the seeds. Chop the tomatoes and mix with the basil, chopped garlic, a little olive oil and a few drops of vinegar. Season with salt and pepper. Divide the mix into two bowls.

2 Cube the avocado flesh and mix with tomatoes in one of the bowls. Cut the baguette into slices and fry in butter until golden brown.

3 Place on kitchen paper. Rub surfaces with the extra clove of garlic and distribute the tomato and tomato/avocado mix on the slices. Serve immediately.

Spinach and Fetta Filo Pastry Parcels

Makes 30 parcels · Preparation and cooking 1 hour 15 minutes

500g (1lb) fresh spinach, stalks removed

5 tablespoons olive oil

½ medium-sized onion, chopped

2 small cloves of garlic, crushed
or chopped

1 small bunch of parsley, finely chopped

1 teaspoon fresh rosemary, chopped
(or 1 teaspoon dried)

1 teaspoon fresh thyme, chopped
(or 1 teaspoon dried)

1 egg

125g (4½oz) fetta cheese, crumbed

salt and freshly ground black pepper

pinch of nutmeg (mace)

parsley to garnish

4 tablespoons butter

125g (4½oz) ready-made filo pastry

1 Rinse the spinach in cold water, squeeze dry in a tea towel, and finely chop. Put the spinach into a dry non-stick frying pan (skillet). Stir on high heat for approximately 2 minutes. In another pan, heat 1 tablespoon of the olive oil and add the onion. Cook gently. Add the garlic and stir for 40 seconds. Stir in all the herbs. Remove the frying pan from the stove. Whip the egg in a bowl and add the crumbed fetta cheese. Add the spinach and season with salt, pepper and nutmeg (mace).

2 To make the parcels, heat 4 tablespoons of olive oil with 4 tablespoons butter on low heat until the butter has melted. Take out one sheet of pastry at a time, keeping the remaining sheets wrapped in a damp tea towel to prevent drying out.

3 Brush a 6 x 6cm (2.5 x 2.5in) pastry square with the butter/oil mixture. Place 1 teaspoon of filling in the middle and fold over one of the edges. Brush. Now fold opposite edge to overlap the first edge. Brush. Fold over a third edge (at right angle) and brush again. Then fold over the last edge, but in the opposite direction downwards, so the filling is covered by the same amount of pastry layers on all sides.

4 Bake the pastries for approximately 30 minutes at 175ºC (155ºC fan, 350ºF, gas 4) until they are golden brown. They can be prepared a day in advance but should be baked just before serving. Decorate with a parsley leaf.

Cheese and Chive Croquettes

Makes 24 · Preparation and cooking 30 minutes + 40 minutes chilling

500g (1lb) mozzarella cheese, grated

185g (6½oz) plain (all-purpose) flour

4 tablespoons fresh chives, finely chopped

½ teaspoon cayenne pepper

2 eggs, lightly beaten

60g (2oz) cornflour (cornstarch)

vegetable oil for deep-frying

1 Place mozzarella cheese, 125g (4½oz) flour, chives, cayenne pepper and eggs in a bowl and mix to combine. Shape mixture into balls, place on a plate lined with plastic wrap and refrigerate for 30 minutes.

2 Combine cornflour (cornstarch) and remaining flour on a plate. Roll balls in flour mixture and refrigerate for 10 minutes.

3 Heat oil in a saucepan (until a cube of bread dropped in browns in 50 seconds) and deep-fry croquettes in batches for 4–5 minutes, or until golden. Drain on absorbent paper and serve.

Meat and Poultry

These recipes, which borrow flavours from both East and West, will satisfy the most demanding carnivores. With the addition of some side dishes, many can be served as main courses, too.

Spanish Chicken Drumettes with Chorizo

Makes 8 small serves · Preparation and cooking 1 hour 20 minutes

8 chicken drumettes

2 tablespoon olive oil

6 spring (green) onions, sliced

2 cloves garlic, crushed

1 red and 1 yellow capsicum (pepper), deseeded and sliced

2 teaspoons paprika

¼ cup dry sherry or dry vermouth

400g (14oz) canned chopped tomatoes

1 bay leaf

1 strip orange zest

75g (2½oz) chorizo, sliced

60g (2oz) pitted black (ripe) olives

salt and freshly ground black pepper to taste

1 Place chicken drumettes in a large, non-stick frying pan (skillet) and fry without oil for 5–8 minutes, turning occasionally, until golden. Remove chicken and set aside, then pour away any fat from the pan. Add oil to the pan and fry spring (green) onions, garlic and capsicum (pepper) for 3–4 minutes, until softened.

2 Return chicken to the pan with the paprika, sherry or vermouth, tomatoes, bay leaf and orange zest. Bring to the boil then simmer covered over a low heat for 35–40 minutes, stirring occasionally until chicken is cooked through.

3 Add chorizo and olives and simmer for a further 5 minutes to heat through, then season with salt and pepper. Serve a drumette with chorizo and pan ingredients into 8 small bowls.

Duck Pancakes

Makes 24 · Preparation and cooking 40 minutes

1 Chinese barbecued duck

24 Chinese pancakes (or burrito tortillas)

4 spring (green) onions, cut into thin 10cm (4in) long pieces

1 Lebanese cucumber, cut into thin 10cm (4in) long pieces

hoisin sauce, to serve

1 Remove skin and meat from duck and slice thinly. Warm pancakes or burritos according to packet directions.

2 Divide duck, spring (green) onions and cucumber evenly between pancakes. Spoon over a little hoisin sauce and fold over pancakes. You may need toothpicks to hold them together for serving. Serve warm.

Chicken Yakitori

Makes 25 skewers · Preparation and cooking 20 minutes + several hours marinating

400g (14oz) skinless chicken breast fillets, sliced 5mm (¼in) thick

½ cup soy sauce

¼ cup honey

1 clove garlic, crushed

½ teaspoon ground ginger

1. Place chicken in a glass bowl, mix in the soy sauce, honey, garlic and ginger. Cover, place in refrigerator and allow to marinate for several hours or overnight.

2. Thread one or two strips onto each skewer (soak skewers in water before use), using a weaving motion. Brush with marinade.

3. Heat grill (broiler) or barbecue to high. Grease rack or plate with oil and arrange the skewers in a row. Cook for 2½ minutes on each side, brushing with marinade as they cook. Serve immediately.

Chicken Empanadas

Makes 15–25 · Preparation and cooking 1 hour

Sour cream pastry

2½ cups plain (all-purpose) flour

pinch of salt

180g (6½oz) butter

1 egg

⅓ cup sour cream

salt and freshly ground black pepper

Filling

1½ tablespoons butter or oil

1 onion, finely chopped

500g (1lb) chicken mince
(ground chicken)

1 cup canned peach slices, chopped finely

1 Sift the flour and salt into a bowl, add butter and rub in with fingertips until like fine breadcrumbs. Mix egg and sour cream together, add to flour mixture and mix to a dough. Wrap in plastic wrap and refrigerate 30 minutes.

2 Heat butter in a pan, add onions and sauté a few minutes. Add chicken and stir while cooking until mince changes colour to white and then to a slightly golden colour. Stir in chopped peach, salt and pepper. Allow to cool.

3 Preheat oven to 200°C (180°C fan, 400°F, gas 6). Roll out dough between 2 sheets of baking paper. Remove top sheet. Cut rounds of pastry about 10–12cm (4–5in) in diameter. Place heaped teaspoon of filling in the centre of each round, moisten edges with water and fold over. Pinch edges well together or press with prongs of a fork. Glaze with milk and bake for 10–15 minutes. Serve hot or cold as finger food, a snack, or a meal with vegetable accompaniments.

Potato Skins

Makes 4 pieces per potato · Preparation and cooking 1 hour

baking potatoes, quantity as desired

125g (4¼oz) butter, melted

salt and freshly ground black pepper

Bacon and mushroom topping

potato pulp

sautéed bacon and mushroom

parsley

Prawn (shrimp) and chives topping

potato pulp

sour cream

fresh chives, chopped

prawns

salt and pepper to taste

Chicken and pine nut topping

potato pulp

cooked chicken

toasted pine nuts

chopped spring (green) onions

sour cream

freshly ground black pepper

1 Preheat the oven to 180°C (160°C fan, 350°F, gas 4). Wash and dry each potato. Pierce with a fork and place in the preheated oven. Bake for 30 minutes or until the centre is firm but can be easily pierced with a fork.

2 Cool the potato, cut in quarters lengthwise and cut out the centre leaving the skin with ½–1cm (¼–½in) of potato on it.

3 Brush the skins with butter, sprinkle them with salt and pepper. Bake them for 10 minutes. Top them with selected topping and bake for another 5–10 minutes, until warmed.

Mini Beef Satays

Makes 24 · Preparation and cooking 50 minutes + 30 minutes marinating

750g (1½lb) lean rump, boneless blade or topside steak

¼ cup white wine

2 teaspoons soy sauce

2 teaspoons satay sauce

¼ teaspoon chilli sauce

1 clove garlic, crushed

1 tablespoon soft brown sugar

1 Soak 24 cocktail bamboo skewers for 30 minutes to prevent burning. Slice meat thinly and evenly into 8cm (3in) long strips. Weave strips onto skewers .

2 Combine wine, sauces, garlic and brown sugar and place in a glass or ceramic dish. Add the meat skewers, turning them in the mixture to coat. Leave to marinate in the mixture for at least 30 minutes, turning occasionally.

3 Place meat skewers on cold grill (broiler) pan – to prevent them sticking during cooking – and cook under pre-heated grill (broiler) for 4–5 minutes each side, basting occasionally with remaining marinade. Garnish with chilli.

Lamb Meatballs with Tzatziki

Makes about 40 · Preparation and cooking 35 minutes + 2 hours draining

450g (15½oz) lamb mince (ground lamb)

1 teaspoon ground coriander

1 teaspoon ground cumin

pinch of chilli

1 tablespoon tomato paste (purée)

⅓ bunch fresh coriander (cilantro), chopped

grated zest of 1 lemon

salt and freshly ground black pepper

oil for frying

Tzatziki

1 continental (English) cucumber, deseeded

500ml (17fl oz) natural yoghurt

1–2 garlic cloves, crushed

1 tablespoon mint, chopped

salt and freshly ground black pepper

1 To make the meatballs, mix all ingredients except the oil together with the lamb and season to taste. Shape the lamb into small meatballs and chill until ready to cook.

2 To make the tzatziki, grate cucumber coarsely, add salt and drain in a colander. Pour the yoghurt into a coffee filter and let drain for a couple of hours. Remove from filter into a bowl, mix yoghurt and cucumber, crushed garlic and chopped mint. Season to taste with salt and pepper.

3 Fry the meatballs in oil until they are cooked through and golden brown. Serve with toothpicks alongside a bowl of tzatziki.

Japanese Pork Gyozas

Makes 22–24 · Preparation and cooking 45 minutes

200g (7oz) pork mince (ground pork)

2 spring (green) onions, sliced

½ cup chopped baby bok choy leaves

2 teaspoons mirin (sweet rice wine)

2 teaspoons light soy sauce

1 teaspoon sesame oil

22–24 gyoza wrappers (Japanese dumpling wrappers)

2–3 tablespoons peanut oil

Dipping sauce

2 tablespoons light soy sauce

2 tablespoons mirin (sweet rice wine)

1 teaspoon ginger (gingerroot), grated

1 Place pork, spring (green) onions, bok choy, mirin (sweet rice wine), soy sauce and sesame oil in a food processor. Process until mixture is combined. Place a heaped teaspoon of mixture in the centre of each gyoza (Japanese dumpling) wrapper. Brush the edges lightly with water and fold over.

2 Place dumpling upright and gently pinch the edges together. Repeat with remaining mixture and wrappers. Line a bamboo steamer with baking paper and make holes in the paper with a skewer. Place steamer over a pan of boiling water.

3 Cook in batches for 6 minutes or until just cooked. Remove and set aside. Heat 2 tablespoons of peanut oil in a frying pan (skillet) over medium heat. Fry dumplings in batches for 1–2 minutes or until crisp.

4 To make the dipping sauce, combine light soy sauce, sweet rice wine and ginger (gingerroot) in a small bowl. Serve dumplings with dipping sauce.

Honey-glazed Spare Ribs

Serves 8 · Preparation and cooking 1 hour + 4 hours marinating

2kg (4lb) pork spare ribs, trimmed of excess fat

2 onions, chopped

2 tablespoons fresh parsley, chopped

1 cup chicken stock (broth)

2 tablespoons lemon juice

125g (4½oz) butter, melted

Honey-soy marinade

4 small fresh red chillies, chopped

4 cloves garlic, chopped

2 spring (green) onions, chopped

1 tablespoon fresh ginger (gingerroot), finely grated

1½ cups rice-wine vinegar

½ cup soy sauce

170g (6oz) honey

1 To make marinade, combine chillies, garlic, spring (green) onions, ginger (gingerroot), vinegar, soy sauce and honey in a non-metallic dish. Add ribs, toss to coat, cover and marinate in the refrigerator for at least 4 hours.

2 Drain ribs and reserve marinade. Cook ribs, basting occasionally with reserved marinade, on a hot barbecue grill for 8–10 minutes or until ribs are tender and golden. Place on a serving platter, cover and keep warm.

3 Place remaining marinade in a saucepan, add onions, parsley, stock (broth) and lemon juice and bring to the boil. Reduce heat and simmer for 15 minutes or until sauce reduces by half. Pour mixture into a food processor or blender and process to make a purée. With motor running, pour in hot melted butter and process to combine. Serve sauce with spare ribs.

Sweetcorn and Ham Croquettes

Makes 16 · Preparation and cooking 40 minutes + 4 hours chilling

½ cup unsalted butter

1 cup plain (all-purpose) flour

1 cup milk

1 cup chicken stock (broth)

1 cup frozen corn kernels (sweetcorn), defrosted

1 cup ham, chopped

1 teaspoon salt

freshly ground black pepper

nutmeg (mace)

1 egg yolk

1 cup plain (all-purpose) flour, extra

2 eggs, beaten

1½ cups breadcrumbs

peanut oil for deep frying

1   Melt butter in a saucepan, add flour and cook stirring constantly until smooth. Add milk and stock (broth), bring to a boil over moderate heat, reduce heat and simmer for 4 minutes, stirring constantly.

2   Stir in corn kernels (sweetcorn) and chopped ham, add salt and season to taste with freshly ground pepper and nutmeg (mace). Cool slightly, then stir in egg yolk.

3   Spread mixture into a square dish, cover and refrigerate until firm, about 4 hours. Divide mixture into squares, dredge in flour, shake off excess and dip in beaten eggs. Finally coat with breadcrumbs.

4   Deep fry croquettes in hot oil until golden. Drain on paper towels. Serve hot.

Seafood

Seafood creates stylish small bites and combines well with different flavours. The influence of Eastern Europe is apparent in the Smoked Salmon Canapés on Rye Bread, while the Greek-inspired Marinated Calamari with Lemon and Herb Dressing could become a meal in itself.

Chermoula Skewers

Makes 24 · Preparation and cooking 35 minutes + 3–4 hours chilling

24 small bamboo skewers

24 green prawns (shrimp), about 750g (1½lb), heads and shells removed

¼ small red onion, roughly chopped

2 garlic cloves, roughly chopped

½ bunch coriander (cilantro) leaves, finely chopped

½ bunch mint leaves, finely chopped

½ bunch continental parsley leaves, finely chopped

1 small red chilli, seeds removed and chopped

1 teaspoon ground cumin

½ teaspoon ground sweet paprika

2 tablespoons lime juice

2 tablespoons olive oil

lime wedges, to serve

1 Soak 24 bamboo skewers in water for 30 minutes. Remove veins from prawns (shrimp) and thread onto skewers. Place prawns in a shallow dish.

2 Place red onion, garlic, coriander (cilantro), mint, parsley, chilli, cumin, paprika, lime juice and olive oil in a food processor. Process until mixture is smooth. Coat prawns in marinade, cover with plastic wrap and place in the fridge for 3–4 hours.

3 Cook prawns on a barbecue or chargrill (broil) for 2–3 minutes or until cooked. Serve prawns with lime wedges.

Teriyaki, Chilli and Ginger Oysters

Makes 24 · Preparation 5 minutes

⅓ cup mirin (sweet rice wine)

2 tablespoons teriyaki sauce

1 medium red chilli, seeds removed and finely chopped

1cm (½in) piece ginger (gingerroot), grated

⅓ bunch chives, sliced

24 oysters

1　Combine mirin (sweet rice wine), teriyaki, chilli, ginger (gingerroot) and chives in a small jug.

2　Place oysters in shell on a serving plate, or remove oysters from shell, and place on Chinese spoons. Drizzle with dressing and serve.

Marinated Calamari with Lemon and Herb Dressing

Serves 4–6 · Preparation and cooking 20 minutes + 3 hours marinating

90ml (3fl oz) lemon juice

3 cloves garlic, crushed

½ cup olive oil, extra for cooking

1kg (2lb) calamari, cut into thin rings and tentacles separated

Dressing

60ml (2fl oz) lemon juice

100ml (3½fl oz) olive oil

1½ tablespoons parsley, chopped

1 garlic clove, crushed

1 teaspoon Dijon mustard

salt and freshly ground black pepper

1 Place lemon juice, garlic and oil in a bowl, add the calamari and marinate for at least 3 hours. If time permits, marinate overnight.

2 To make the dressing, place all ingredients in a bowl or jar and whisk well (until the dressing thickens slightly).

3 Heat 1 tablespoon of oil in a pan, add the calamari and cook for a few minutes, until calamari are cooked through. Alternatively, the calamari can be cooked on a chargrill plate (broiler). Serve calamari with lemon and herb dressing drizzled over.

Crab Rice Paper Rolls

Makes about 22 · Preparation and cooking 35 minutes

60g (2oz) vermicelli noodles

1 Lebanese cucumber, halved lengthwise and seeds removed

4 spring (green) onions, thinly sliced

½ bunch coriander (cilantro), leaves picked

½ bunch fresh mint, leaves picked

300g (10½oz) fresh crab meat

¼ cup lemon juice

2 tablespoons sweet-chilli sauce

22 small rice paper sheets about 16cm (6in) round

Dipping sauce

¼ cup sweet-chilli sauce

2 tablespoons rice vinegar

2 teaspoons fish sauce

1 Cook noodles in a saucepan of boiling water for 3–4 minutes or until tender. Drain and set aside. Cut cucumber in half again lengthwise and thinly slice.

2 Combine noodles, spring (green) onions, cucumber, coriander (cilantro), mint, crab meat, lemon juice and sweet-chilli sauce in a bowl. Dip each rice paper sheet in a bowl of very hot water (nearly boiling) until soft. Place four at a time on a clean surface. Place spoonfuls of mixture on the sheets, fold in the edges and roll up. Repeat with remaining mixture and sheets.

3 To make the dipping sauce, combine sweet-chilli sauce, rice vinegar and fish sauce in a small bowl.

Fish Cakes

Makes 24 · Preparation and cooking 50 minutes

500g (1lb) boneless white fish fillets, roughly chopped

2 spring (green) onions, sliced

¼ bunch coriander (cilantro), freshly chopped

1 tablespoon red curry paste (jerk seasoning)

2 teaspoons fish sauce

1 tablespoon cornflour (cornstarch)

1 egg

2–3 tablespoons peanut oil

lime wedges to garnish

Dipping sauce

¼ cup sweet-chilli sauce

2 tablespoons lemon juice

1 teaspoon fish sauce

1 Place fish, spring (green) onions, coriander (cilantro), curry paste (jerk seasoning), fish sauce, cornflour (cornstarch) and egg in a food processor. Process until mixture is combined. Using wet hands, shape tablespoons of the mixture into 24 cakes.

2 Place cakes on a plate, cover with plastic wrap and place in the fridge for 30 minutes. Heat 2 tablespoons of oil in a heavy non-stick frying pan (skillet). Cook fish cakes in batches for 1–2 minutes each side or until golden.

3 To make the dipping sauce, combine sweet-chilli sauce, lemon juice and fish sauce in a small bowl. Serve fish cakes with dipping sauce. Garnish with lime wedges.

Smoked Salmon Canapés

Makes 24 · Preparation 10 minutes

⅓ cup cream cheese

1 tablespoon horseradish cream

1 tablespoon chives, thinly sliced

6 slices rye bread, cut into quarters

200g (7oz) smoked salmon, sliced

baby capers to garnish

1　Combine cream cheese, horseradish cream and chives in a small bowl.

2　Spread bread evenly with cream cheese mixture. Top with smoked salmon and garnish with capers.

Pastry Cases with Sweet-chilli Crab

Makes 20–25 · Preparation 10 minutes

250g (8oz) light cream cheese

170g (6oz) canned crab meat, drained

1 tablespoon lime juice

1 tablespoon sweet-chilli sauce

1 tablespoon fresh chives, sliced

20–25 packaged savoury pastry cases

extra chives, sliced to garnish

1 Place cream cheese, crab meat, lime juice, sweet-chilli sauce and chives in a food processor. Process until combined.

2 Place pastry cases on a serving plate. Spoon crab mixture into cases and sprinkle with extra chives.

Desserts

A mouthful of something sweet is always welcome at the end of a party. Most desserts can be made to bite-size proportions, and fruit is nature's perfect finger food, whether in a mini tartlet, as a kebab or dipped in chocolate.

Brandy Apricot Slice

Makes 16 · Preparation and cooking 55 minutes

½ cup dried apricots, chopped

2 tablespoons brandy

100g (3½oz) dark (semi-sweet) chocolate

4 tablespoons butter

3 tablespoons milk

1 egg

¼ cup caster (berry) sugar

¾cup plain (all-purpose) flour, sifted

¼ teaspoon baking powder

Chocolate icing (frosting)

50g (1¾oz) dark (semi-sweet) chocolate

1 tablespoon milk

1½ cups icing (confectioner's)
sugar, sifted

1 tablespoon butter

1 Combine apricots and brandy, set aside for 15 minutes. Melt chocolate and butter together, stir in the milk, egg, sugar, flour and baking powder. Mix well. Stir the apricots through the chocolate mixture.

2 Spoon mixture into a lightly greased 20cm (8in) square sandwich pan. Bake at 180ºC (160ºC fan, 350ºF, gas 4) for 12–15 minutes or until firm. Cool in the tin. Ice (frost) with chocolate icing.

3 To make the chocolate icing, melt together chocolate and milk, blend in icing (confectioner's) sugar and butter. Mix well. Garnish with diced apricots.

Fruit Tartlets

Makes 18 · Preparation and cooking 1 hour 15 minutes + chilling

Pastry

1½ cups plain (all-purpose) flour

2 tablespoons icing (confectioner's) sugar

125g (4½oz) butter

2 egg yolks

1 teaspoon water, approximately

Custard cream

2 eggs

1 egg yolk

½ cup white (granulated) sugar

1½ tablespoon cornflour (cornstarch)

¾ cup milk

¼ cup cream

1 tablespoon Grand Marnier

Topping

1 teaspoon gelatine

⅓ cup water

½ cup apricot jam (jelly)

2 teaspoons Grand Marnier

12 strawberries, halved or sliced

1 cup grapes (green or black), halved

2 kiwifruit, sliced

425g (15oz) can apricot halves, drained and sliced

2 peaches, sliced

1 Preheat the oven to 190ºC (170ºC fan, 375ºF, gas 5).

2 To make the pastry: sift flour and icing (confectioner's) sugar into a bowl and rub in butter. Add egg yolk and enough water to make ingredients cling together. Knead on lightly floured surface until smooth.

3 Divide mixture into 12 equal portions, roll each portion to fit shallow patty pans or small fluted flan tins. Prick pastry all over with a fork. Bake in the oven for 10 minutes or until golden brown. Cool.

4 To make the custard cream, whisk eggs and egg yolk, sugar and cornflour (cornstarch) in a bowl until thick. Heat milk and cream in a saucepan, gradually whisk in egg mixture. Whisk over low heat until thickened (do not boil). Stir in Grand Marnier. Cover and cool.

5 To make the topping, sprinkle gelatine over water, stir, dissolve over pan of simmering water. Heat apricot jam (jelly) in a small saucepan, strain, stir in Grand Marnier and gelatine mixture, then cool until beginning to thicken.

6 To assemble, spread custard cream evenly into pastry cases. Arrange fruit in a decorative pattern over custard. Brush fruit with apricot glaze. Refrigerate until firm.

Double-dipped Chocolate Strawberries

Makes about 25 · Preparation 30 minutes + chilling

125g (4½oz) white chocolate

60g (2oz) copha (vegetable shortening)

500g (1lb) strawberries

125g (4½oz) dark (semi-sweet) chocolate

1 Melt white chocolate with half the copha (vegetable shortening) in a bowl over saucepan of simmering water.

2 Hold strawberries by the stem, dip $^2/_3$ of the strawberry into chocolate. Hold over chocolate to allow excess to run off. Place onto a foil covered tray, refrigerate until set.

3 Melt dark chocolate with remaining copha in a bowl over a saucepan of simmering water.

4 Dip strawberries into chocolate, $^2/_3$ of the way up the white chocolate. Hold over chocolate to allow excess to run off. Place onto foil covered tray, refrigerate until set.

Baby Florentines

Makes about 40 · Preparation and cooking 1 hour 5 minutes

¼ cup white (granulated) sugar

1¾ tablespoons unsalted butter

1¼ tablespoons honey

1¼ tablespoons cream

⅓ cup slivered almonds

1½ tablespoons glacé (glazed) orange zest, chopped

1½ tablespoons glacé (glazed) cherries, chopped

125g (4½oz) dark (semi-sweet) chocolate, chopped

1 In a saucepan combine sugar, butter, honey and cream. Bring to the boil over moderate heat, boil 5 minutes, stirring constantly. Add almonds, orange zest and cherries. Allow mixture to cool 5 minutes.

2 Preheat oven to 200°C (180°C fan, 400°F, gas 6). Line baking trays (sheets) with baking paper. Spoon ½ teaspoons onto baking tray, 5cm (2in) apart. Bake for 5 minutes in the middle of oven. Remove from oven and, if desired, trim edges into a neat shape. Return to oven and bake a further 4 minutes, until biscuits (wafers) are golden and bubbly.

3 Remove baking trays from oven and let biscuits cool for 2 minutes. Remove from sheets with a spatula, cool on wire racks. If biscuits become too hard and set to remove, return to oven for 1 minute to slightly soften.

4 Melt chocolate in a bowl set over hot water. Remove from heat. Brush a thin layer of chocolate onto the smooth underside of the wafers. When dry, brush with a second layer.

5 Use a fork to drizzle zig zag patterns of chocolate onto the tops of the biscuits. Allow chocolate to cool. Store in an airtight container in the refrigerator.

Chocolate Pecan Brownies

Makes 24 squares · Preparation and cooking 1 hour 10 minutes

1½ cups pecan nuts

½ cup plain (all-purpose) flour, sifted

¼ cup white (granulated) sugar

½ cup dark glucose (corn) syrup

90g (3oz) dark (semi-sweet) chocolate, chopped

45g (1½oz) butter

2 eggs, lightly beaten

1 tablespoon rum

1 tablespoon icing (confectioner's) sugar

1 Preheat oven to a moderate temperature. Chop pecans finely by hand (a food processor is unsuitable). Combine pecans and flour in a bowl.

2 Combine sugar and syrup in a saucepan, stir over heat until boiling. Remove from heat, add chocolate and butter, stir until chocolate has melted and mixture is smooth. Add the eggs and rum and stir until combined.

3 Add this mixture to the flour and pecans and stir until combined.

4 Grease a 19 x 29 x 3.5cm (7.5 x 11.5 x 1.5in) baking tray (sheet), line base and sides with greased paper. Spread mixture evenly into tray. Bake in moderate oven for about 30 minutes or until set.

5 Cool in pan for 10 minutes before turning onto wire rack to cool. Dust with sifted icing (confectioner's) sugar, cut into small squares and serve.

Profiteroles

Makes about 20 · Preparation and cooking 1 hour 15 minutes

1 cup water

4 tablespoons butter

1 cup plain (all-purpose) flour

3 eggs, beaten

whipped cream

Chocolate sauce

200g (7oz) dark (semi-sweet) chocolate

⅓ cup unthickened (half and half) cream

1 Preheat oven to 200°C (180°C fan, 400°F, gas 6).

2 Place water and butter in a saucepan and cook over gentle heat until butter has melted and water boils. Remove from heat, add the sifted flour and stir vigorously.

3 Return to heat and stir continuously until mixture forms a ball around the spoon. Cool. Gradually beat in the eggs, beating well between each addition.

4 Place teaspoons of mixture onto greased baking trays (sheets) and sprinkle trays with cold water. Bake at 200°C (180°C fan, 400°F, gas 6) for 10 minutes, reduce heat to 180°C (160°C fan, 350°F, gas 4) and continue to cook for a further 30 minutes or until puffs are golden and feel light in the hand. Pierce puffs to allow steam to escape. Allow to cool.

5 To make the chocolate sauce, melt chocolate over boiling water, stir in cream and mix until smooth.

6 Fill profiteroles with whipped cream and serve drizzled with chocolate sauce.

Fruit Skewers with Honey Cream

Serves 4 · Preparation 15 minutes

1 punnet strawberries, about 250g (8oz)

1 small rockmelon (canteloupe)

4 kiwifruit

Honey cream

1 cup sour cream

1 cup thickened (whipping) cream

2 tablespoons honey

2 tablespoons chopped fresh mint

1 Peel the fruit and cut into bite-sized pieces. Thread onto bamboo skewers or toothpicks.

2 To make the honey cream, combine sour cream, cream, honey and mint. Serve with fruit skewers for dipping.

Chocolate Rum Pudding

Serves 6–8 · Preparation and cooking 1 hour 15 minutes

¾ cup sultanas (golden raisins)

1 tablespoon rum

200g (7oz) dark (semi-sweet) chocolate-covered biscuits (cookies)

1½ cups self-raising flour

125g (4½oz) butter, melted

2 eggs

¾ cup milk

1 Soak sultanas (golden raisins) in rum for 30 minutes. Place biscuits (cookies) into food processor, process until fine. Combine with flour in a bowl, making a well in the centre.

2 Beat together melted butter, eggs and milk. Pour into centre of well with sultanas and rum mixture. Stir until just mixed through. Spoon into eight greased muffin or brioche pans. Bake in 180ºC (160ºC fan, 350ºF, gas 4) oven for 25–30 minutes. Serve plain, or warm with cream, custard and/or chocolate sauce.

Weights and Measures

Weights and measures differ from country to country, but with these handy conversion charts cooking has never been easier!

Cup Measurements

One cup of these commonly used ingredients is equal to the following weights.

Ingredient	Metric	Imperial
Apples (dried and chopped)	125g	4½oz
Apricots (dried and chopped)	190g	6¾oz
Breadcrumbs (packet)	125g	4½oz
Breadcrumbs (soft)	55g	2oz
Butter	225g	8oz
Cheese (shredded/grated)	115g	4oz
Choc bits	155g	5½oz
Coconut (desiccated/fine)	90g	3oz
Flour (plain/all-purpose, self-raising)	115g	4oz
Fruit (dried)	170g	6oz
Golden (corn) syrup	315g	11oz
Honey	315g	11oz
Margarine	225g	8oz
Nuts (chopped)	115g	4oz
Rice (cooked)	155g	5½oz
Rice (uncooked)	225g	8oz
Sugar (brown)	155g	5½oz
Sugar (caster/berry/superfine)	225g	8oz
Sugar (granulated)	225g	8oz
Sugar (sifted, icing/confectioner's)	155g	5½oz
Treacle (molasses)	315g	11oz

Oven Temperatures

Celsius	Fahrenheit	Gas mark
120	250	1
150	300	2
160	320	3
180	350	4
190	375	5
200	400	6
220	430	7
230	450	8
250	480	9

Liquid Measures

Cup	Metric	Imperial
¼ cup	63ml	2¼fl oz
½ cup	125ml	4½fl oz
¾ cup	188ml	6⅔fl oz
1 cup	250ml	8¾fl oz
1¾ cup	438ml	15½fl oz
2 cups	500ml	17½fl oz
4 cups	1 litre	35fl oz

Spoon	Metric	Imperial
¼ teaspoon	1.25ml	1/25fl oz
½ teaspoon	2.5ml	1/12fl oz
1 teaspoon	5ml	1/6fl oz
1 tablespoon	15ml	½fl oz

Weight Measures

Metric	Imperial
10g	¼oz
15g	½oz
20g	¾oz
30g	1oz
60g	2oz
115g	4oz (¼lb)
125g	4½oz
145g	5oz
170g	6oz
185g	6½oz
200g	7oz
225g	8oz (½lb)
300g	10½oz
330g	11½oz
370g	13oz
400g	14oz
425g	15oz
455g	16oz (1lb)
500g	17½oz (1lb 1½oz)
600g	21oz (1lb 5oz)
650g	23oz (1lb 7oz)
750g	26½oz (1lb 10½oz)
1000g (1kg)	35oz (2lb 3oz)

Index